OIL ENERGY

PUTTING OIL TO WORK

COOK MEMORIAL LIBRARY DISTRICT
413 N. MILWAUKEE AVE.
LIBERTYVILLE, ILLINOIS 60048

JESSIE ALKIRE

Consulting Editor, Diane Craig, M.A./Reading Specialist

Super Sandcastle

An Imprint of Abdo Publishing
abdopublishing.com

abdopublishing.com

Published by Abdo Publishing, a division of ABDO, PO Box 398166, Minneapolis, Minnesota 55439. Copyright © 2019 by Abdo Consulting Group, Inc. International copyrights reserved in all countries. No part of this book may be reproduced in any form without written permission from the publisher. Super SandCastle™ is a trademark and logo of Abdo Publishing.

Printed in the United States of America, North Mankato, Minnesota

052018
092018

Design and Production: Mighty Media, Inc.
Editor: Megan Borgert-Spaniol
Cover Photographs: Shutterstock; Wikimedia Commons
Interior Photographs: iStockphoto; Mighty Media, Inc.; Shutterstock; Wikimedia Commons

Library of Congress Control Number: 2017961855

Publisher's Cataloging-in-Publication Data
Names: Alkire, Jessie, author.
Title: Oil energy: Putting oil to work / by Jessie Alkire.
Other titles: Putting oil to work
Description: Minneapolis, Minnesota : Abdo Publishing, 2019. | Series: Earth's
    energy innovations
Identifiers: ISBN 9781532115738 (lib.bdg.) | ISBN 9781532156458 (ebook)
Subjects: LCSH: Petroleum as fuel--Juvenile literature. | Power resources--
    Juvenile literature. | Energy development--Juvenile literature. | Energy
    conversion--Juvenile literature.
Classification: DDC 553.28--dc23

Super SandCastle™ books are created by a team of professional educators, reading specialists, and content developers around five essential components—phonemic awareness, phonics, vocabulary, text comprehension, and fluency—to assist young readers as they develop reading skills and strategies and increase their general knowledge. All books are written, reviewed, and leveled for guided reading, early reading intervention, and Accelerated Reader™ programs for use in shared, guided, and independent reading and writing activities to support a balanced approach to literacy instruction.

CONTENTS

What Is Oil Energy? 4

Energy Timeline 6

Oil Boom 8

Gasoline 10

Oil Issues 12

Everyday Fuel 14

Drilling for Oil 16

Refined into Fuel 18

Uncertain Future 20

More About Oil Energy 22

Test Your Knowledge 23

Glossary 24

WHAT IS OIL ENERGY?

Oil energy is energy created from burning oil. Oil is a **fossil fuel**. It forms from the remains of plants and animals. Heat and pressure change these remains to oil. This process takes millions of years!

Oil is used to make fuels. But it is nonrenewable. The world is slowly using up its oil supply.

Oil flowing from well

Oil is sometimes pumped from underground using devices called pump jacks.

ENERGY TIMELINE

480 BCE

Persians use oil to make flaming arrows.

1100s CE

Oil is burned for light.

1859

Edwin Drake drills the first successful US oil well.

Discover how oil energy has changed over time!

1900s

Oil is processed into **gasoline** to power cars.

1970s

The United States depends on the Middle East for oil.

2016

The United States uses 391 million gallons (1.5 billion L) of gasoline each day.

OIL BOOM

Persians fighting Greeks in the Battle of Plataea

People have used oil for thousands of years. Ancient Egyptians used it in medicines. Persians used oil around 480 BCE. They dipped arrows in oil. Then the arrows were set on fire and shot at enemies. By the 1100s CE, oil was burned for light.

Edwin Drake drilled an oil well in 1859. Other people used Drake's methods. Oil's popularity boomed!

EDWIN DRAKE

BORN: March 29, 1819, Greenville, New York

DIED: November 8, 1880, Bethlehem, Pennsylvania

Edwin Drake drilled the first successful US oil well. Drake met with an oil company in 1857. It wanted to get oil for lighting. The company hired Drake to drill an oil well in Titusville, Pennsylvania. Drake finished drilling in 1859. The well reached 69 feet (21 m) deep!

GASOLINE

By the early 1900s, people were using electric light bulbs. Oil was no longer preferred for light. But oil had a new purpose. Oil was processed into **gasoline**. Gasoline powered cars!

Gasoline powered the 1910 Ford Model T.

The United States was using a lot of oil. But its oil supplies were limited. Much of the nation's oil came from the Middle East.

Saudi Arabia, Iran, and Iraq are top oil producers in the Middle East.

OIL ISSUES

Oil is a common energy **resource** today. But many nations must get their oil from other countries. This can create conflict.

Oil also affects the **environment**. Drilling and **transporting** oil can cause oil spills. Burning oil produces **greenhouse gases**. Scientists work to reduce oil's harmful effects.

Offshore oil rig fire

Oil spills pollute water. They also harm sea life.

13

EVERYDAY FUEL

Most oil is used to make **gasoline**. Cars and other **vehicles** run on this fuel. The United States used 391 million gallons (1.5 billion L) of gasoline each day in 2016!

Oil is also made into other fuels. These fuels power trucks and airplanes. They are also burned to produce heat and electricity.

Gasoline pump

Airplanes are powered by a special oil product called jet fuel.

DRILLING FOR OIL

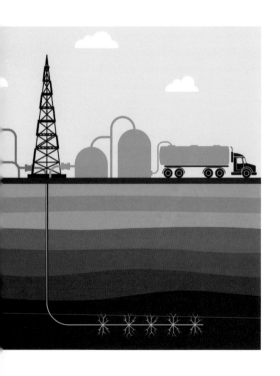

Oil fracking site

Oil rises from deep underground. Most oil gets trapped underneath rock layers. This forms an oil **reservoir**. Scientists help find rock layers that hold trapped oil.

Workers drill into oil reservoirs. Then they pump oil to the surface. Drillers also use a method called fracking. They pump high-pressure water underground. This breaks rock that is trapping oil.

Oil wells are drilled on dry land and offshore in the ocean.
Oil platforms are built to support offshore oil wells.

REFINED INTO FUEL

Oil refinery

Crude oil is **refined** into different fuels. The oil is heated. It turns into liquid and vapor. Then it separates in a tower. Lighter fuels rise to the top of the tower. Heavier ones fall to the bottom.

The fuels are processed further. Then they are ready to power **vehicles**, buildings, and more!

OIL SEPARATION TOWER

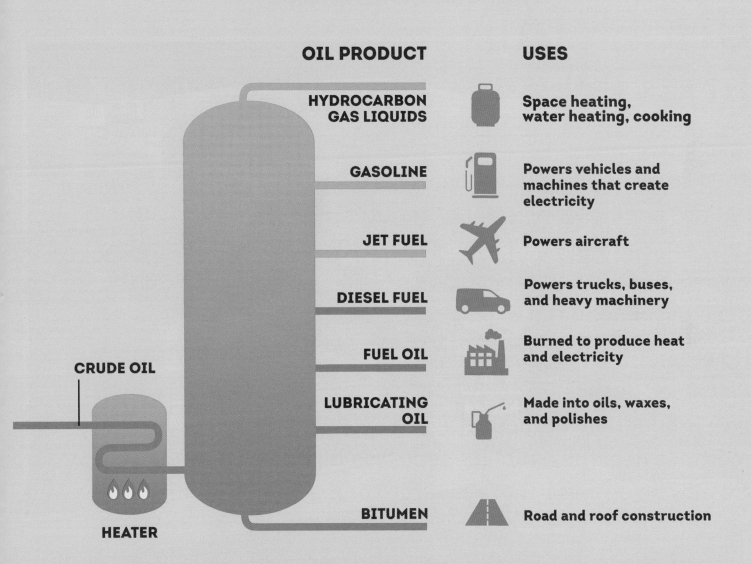

OIL PRODUCT

USES

HYDROCARBON GAS LIQUIDS — Space heating, water heating, cooking

GASOLINE — Powers vehicles and machines that create electricity

JET FUEL — Powers aircraft

DIESEL FUEL — Powers trucks, buses, and heavy machinery

FUEL OIL — Burned to produce heat and electricity

LUBRICATING OIL — Made into oils, waxes, and polishes

BITUMEN — Road and roof construction

CRUDE OIL

HEATER

UNCERTAIN FUTURE

The **future** of oil is uncertain. Many nations are exploring cleaner, renewable energies. People are also buying electric cars. These do not need **gasoline** to run.

Electric car charging

However, US oil production has increased. Engineers search for new production methods. These methods help the nation depend less on other countries. Oil may be an important **resource** for many more years!

Nearly half of all US oil is produced in Texas and North Dakota.

MORE ABOUT OIL ENERGY

Do you want to tell others about oil energy? Here are some fun facts to share!

OIL IS MOSTLY MADE OF the elements hydrogen and carbon.

PRODUCTS SUCH AS tires, footballs, and paint are made of oil.

OIL IS MEASURED in barrels. One barrel is about 42 gallons (159 L).

TEST YOUR KNOWLEDGE

1. Oil is a **fossil fuel**.
   TRUE OR FALSE?

2. When did Edwin Drake finish drilling the first successful US oil well?

3. What oil product powers cars?

THINK ABOUT IT!

Does your family's car run on **gasoline**? This is oil energy at work!

ANSWERS: 1. True 2. 1859 3. Gasoline

GLOSSARY

crude oil – natural oil that has not been refined.

environment – nature and everything in it, such as the land, sea, and air.

fossil fuel – a fuel formed from the remains of plants or animals. Coal, oil, and natural gas are fossil fuels.

future – the time that hasn't happened yet.

gasoline – a liquid that can burn that is used to power engines.

greenhouse gas – a gas, such as carbon dioxide, that traps heat in Earth's atmosphere.

refine – to remove unwanted parts of something to make it usable or valuable.

reservoir – a natural or human-made place where something is stored.

resource – something that is usable or valuable.

transport – to move something from one place to another.

vehicle – something used to carry persons or large objects. Examples include cars, trucks, and buses.